LIVE LOVE LIFE, A POETIC SYMPHONY FROM ONE'S HEART

Live Love Life, A Poetic Symphony from One's Heart

Edonusem H.A.Y. Pomeyie

ONION RIVER PRESS

DEDICATION

To God almighty for being my Strength, and wisdom,

To my twin in Heaven Edomdedzie, Thanks for being my Muse, my inspiration and the voice within my Struggle.

To my mother, my guide, and helper who has been there through thick and thin.

To my father, my challenger who challenged me to be better.

To both my African and American families for being the pillars that I lean on.

Lastly to all the poets of the future, never give up on telling your truth.

CONTENTS

FOREWORD

I still remember the first time Edonusem stood before the class to share one of his poems. There was something undeniably honest in his voice, something raw, tender, and wise beyond his years. As a teacher, you hope to spark a love for words in your students, but every so often, you come across a student who doesn't just learn the craft, they live it.

From his earliest works in middle school, Edonusem displayed a rare ability to take emotion, whether joy, anger, sorrow, or love, and create it into language that others could feel deeply. Edonusem's writing always stood out, not because it followed all the rules, but because it had something genuine to say. His poetry reflected thoughtfulness, depth, and a willingness to explore difficult topics. He really made his work memorable with his commitment to using poetry as a way to express emotion and ideas clearly and honestly.

In *Live Love Life: A Poetic Symphony From One's Heart*, Edonusem takes that same honesty and brings it into a new phase of maturity. These poems are not written for performance or to fit a mold, they're personal reflections on love, loss, struggle, identity, and the many experiences that shape who we are.

This collection doesn't try to be polished in the conventional sense. It's more interested in being real, and that's what gives it power. There's a freedom in this kind of writing, a refusal to be boxed in by structure or expectation. What results is a series of poems that speak directly from the author's life to the reader. He has built his own poetic voice that is inspiring, and he writes not to impress, but to express. He chooses vulnerability over silence, emotion over expectation, and truth over convenience.

It's been rewarding to see how Edonusem has continued writing over the years, building on what he learned in the classroom while also allowing his style to evolve. I'm proud to see this new collection come to life, and I hope readers take the time to sit with these poems, not just to read them, but to really hear them.

Mrs. Kara Beste
August 2025

INTRODUCTION

POETIC VIEW OF POETRY

Mom once asked me "what type of poems do you write?" She was shocked that I didn't know, as she started to talk about sonnets. I further explained to her that I am disinterested about types of poems because "poetry isn't supposed to make sense, it is supposed to make you feel". Once poetry has a type/structure it makes sense from the social or societal point of view (It has a label). While poetry is a singular personal experience. Which anyone can accomplish no matter if they have the structure or not. There is no structure for emotion, hence no structure for the emotional. There is a general knowledge that poetry must follow a structure, but I disagree, and it does not dictate my path of writing. Subsequently if poetry does not have emotion, it doesn't have the flavor, or spice to make it a great poem. So, to me, my poetry is my voice, it is my choice, and it's not structured. From my experiences I only write great poems when something big inspires me or when an emotional event has happened. When this occurs, I drop everything and write. When I can't hold in my feelings anymore,

I pour it all on my computer so that my words can resonate and guide when read. Due to this when in school or wherever others can tell when I'm in my "poetic zone". Cause usually I would be typing about whether in the hall, in the kitchen, on the floor, on the toilet, or in class. All this with my air pods in, and my words flowing onto the computer page with the occasional head nod to whatever song that fits my mood. "We don't read and write poetry because it's cute. We Read and write poetry because we are members of the human race. And medicine, law, business, engineering, these are noble pursuits and necessary to sustain life. But poetry, beauty, romance, love, these are what we stay alive for" (Dead Poets Society John Keeting). Additionally, I believe poetry is like a symphony. Our words have the power to change minds, hearts, and souls. Because of this we have the power to change the world just like music. With this poetic point of view on poetry let us create a Symphony that will resonate in history. Let us create poetry together. Me and you, us and them, For the better. I hope you get inspired to create your own poetry after reading this book to help build on our world culture, future, and power. From one Poet to another, let us change the world as we pursue community, unity, equity, and poetry.

8TH GRADE

These sets of poems were written in my 8th grade English class. Most were influenced by the lesson of the day and the theme of my assignment my English teacher Mrs. Beste gave us. Occasionally I would write poems influenced by emotions like "Tired Anger poem" for example. This poem was written while I had a fever. My 8th grade year was a year of poetic growth for me. I figured out new rhymes through the Rhyme Zone website. Additionally, I wrote bird themed sets of poems when I got a poetic realization of humanities similarities to birds characteristics. Some of my favorite poems were written in 8th grade. This includes "True Blue Bass Poem", "Microphone Poem", and many more. I hope these poems speak to your heart as they did me, when I was going through a process of self-discovery. I would call this grade my poetic exploration.

MICROPHONE POEM

As my eyes blink open my voice jumps high letting my power rise. As people hold me, they think of the past, my bravery on stage bringing the best in anyone.

My wings are my voice louder and louder I sing while I dance to my own song. As I cook up feeling I make people cry as I cook up feeling I make people sigh.

I remember boys and girls, men and women young and old closing their eyes while I open mine for my talented wings in life drive people to perfection. My life is not all jolly.

I screech when I am tired, I break when I am sad, but I bring the best in people. I dream as I sing, I am a microphone.

STOPPING BY WOODS ON A SNOWY DAWN

Walking through the woods I go.
The snow piles up like a mound of dough.
The trees seem like they glow.
I know that my life will grow.

I watch till I go so slow.
Watching the water flow.
Suddenly I see a black crow.
Landing so swiftly on a snowy branch like a pro.

The sun rises, shining bright.
The Stars disappear bringing new daylight.
My woods are such a beautiful sight.
My loud cry gives me might.
As my new journey will start tonight.

Though the cold may bring fright.
My soul will feel so upright.

I ignited a fire so uptight.
That my fingers are so cold from frostbite.

9/ 11 POEM: THE DAY OF DARKNESS AND LIGHT

There was a day of evil and there was a glimpse of light.

This light shined blue, white, and red. I was not alive to see this light shine. I was not alive to see it's flight.

But the light of my heart and of others shines like how it shined with bravery, hope, life, and kindness.

9/11 the day of darkness and light, the day of death and life. Hope rains in the form of flowing water and in a single tree surviving that day we should remember as the day of light.

There was terror, chaos, sadness, anger, bloodshed, and loss. Why sacrifice your life for destruction? Why does darkness try to overtake us and surround us with the fog of sadness?

But there is light in bravery, light in bravery, light and kindness, and what the enemy plans for evil turns to good. For this chaos brought us together in the morning, to our brothers and sisters who died for light.

INSPIRED BY LANGSTON HUGHES

WHAT HAPPENS TO A DREAM DEFERRED

Does it Pierce the hearts of many like an arrow through the sky, or does it split like an old garment destroyed from years? Does it burn like paper tossed and forgotten in the fire of the past, or does it melt like wax in the sun of day? Maybe it snaps like a bracelet worn out by the years forgotten by its owner, or maybe it breaks on a rock so sharp sticking out of sand so deep.

WHAT HAPPENS TO A DREAM FULFILLED

Does it shine like the sun on a cool summer day, or does it open the door of love that defeats all darkness? Does it fly like a dove soaring through the sky to find a home, or does it sparkle like the evening stars that lull you to sleep? Maybe it grows like a maple tree that will blossom and bring sweet syrup to your plate, or maybe it fills you up with joy like a flowing fountain that has no limits? My dream will strengthen and lift others' hearts like God's mighty hand that overcomes all evil.

SOUL FALL HAIKU

Falling is the leaves,

Swiftly the wind blows through me,

Red is in the trees.

THE PICTURE IN THEE HAIKU

Pollen falling high,

Crunching through the leaves I go,

Grass swaying slowly.

I AM GOING OUT POEM: GRAINS OF LIFE

I'm going out to the grain field.

I will only wait for the blue jay's song.

And watch as the bees buzz and talk.

I won't be long. I only wish that you would come and
dance along.

I AM GOING OUT POEM: MIGHTY HAPPINESS

I'm going to the mudslide.

I will only wait for my Grandchild's smile.

And watch as the Hawks fly.

I won't be long, I only wish that you may join and laugh with me.

INSPIRED BY WILLIAM CARLOS WILLIAMS

SO MUCH DEPENDS UPON A TEDDY BEAR

So much depends upon,
A bear made with love and care,
Hugged all night,
In the cozy bed.

SO MUCH DEPENDS UPON A PHOTO ALBUM

So much depends Upon,
A book of memories and pictures,
Shared with others who are dear,
On a bookstand,
In the Livingroom.

SO MUCH DEPENDS UPON A BASKETBALL

So much depends upon,
A ball of light and hope,
Through the net with strength and ease,
While people laugh with tender care.

PINK WHITE BOW

In loving memory of Edomdedzi Henritta Pomeyie
(my sister)

When I Look upon my broken past,

I see a pink white bow.

Now strewn with dust but used with trust.

I see how my heart was crushed.

Past forgotten in a desk now remembered with love and
care.

POETRY IS A METAPHOR POEM

Poetry is a tree,

With leaves, and branches so tall,

Each planting its own seed,

Each growing at its own pace,

Making a world of feelings,

We can't breathe without,

Making each reader stand tall in the wild storm.

POETRY IS A METAPHOR POEM

Poetry is candy,

With colors so bright,

Each with its own taste of feelings,

Each with words that fill your mind with knowledge,

Each stirring its own ingredients of wisdom,

Making each reader Complete.

TIGER POEM

Tiger,

Patient, Wise,

Running, Hunting,

On the Island,

Cute, Terrifying,

Jumping, Sleeping,

In Hiding.

ANIMAL POEM LION

Beside the clear water,
The Lion awakes,
Still tired,
The beast roars,
Ready for his day.
Blinking slowly,
He walks his way,
Like a majestic king,
Through the jungle.
He greets his kingdom,
With a song,
Singing louder and louder,
As the birds fly away.
Now spotting a Zebra,
He blends with the scene,
Now ready to pounce,
He makes his declare,
With a Hungry growl,
He kills his prey.
Feasting Happily,
With patience and ease.

ANIMAL POEM DOVE

Through the sky,
A dove flies high,
Looking happily,
He spots a Branch.
Majestic and cool,
He makes a sound,
So lovely and true,
But not his own.
Curious and memorized,
He makes his way,
Dancing through the dense green forest.
Meeting his friend,
They laugh and play,
Enjoying each other's company.
Now the sun comes down,
While the night approaches,
Saying goodbye,
The dove climbs high.
With his graceful claws,
He builds a nest,
Ready for a good night's sleep.

BALD EAGLE POEM

Dangerous, Cruel,

Flies Rapidly,

Kills cleverly,

Through the sky.

Eats cautiously,

Lands swiftly,

In the nest.

Brave Almighty Ruler of Birds

POEMS FROM THE HEART

1 WHAT MAKES US WHO WE ARE WINGS (TALENTS)

Wings help you to fly,
Help you to glide through the skies,
Let your wings fly high,
Let all the world know that your wings are special,
with talents and hard work put in your vessel,
For without your wings you can't sing, be king, or be
willing to bring spring.
Let your wings dance like they are hearing a song, or
they are playing ping - pong, for they are not wrong to
think that there is life in dancing,
Oh, Let your wings guide,
for it is not bad to rely,
It is not bad to fly high,
It is not bad to be fly,
Cause people try,
To bring you down from up high,
Whether you got your wings or not
So, keep flying to the mountains,
To the oceans,
To everywhere,

And see that your wings are your talents, and your talents make who you are beautiful.

2 WHAT MAKES US WHO WE ARE CLAWS (PERSONALITY)

We all have claws,
Our Claws can be our flaws,
Too sharp to the point of hurt,
Feeling like you are an introvert,
Are you wearing a shirt, skirt, or becoming an extrovert,
Our claws can be short to the point that we can´t hold
on,
It feels like we are going to fall,
Or we just pretend we are up in the air playing basket-
ball,
All in all, being tall is not a flaw,
Just be yourself and you will be great,
Being great takes heart,
Sometimes it takes a restart,
To become a pop tart, you need to be great,
Life is hard,
Try not to guard your heart,
What is most important is being yourself,
Your personality is your mentality,
Being great should be your nationality,
Gravity pulls you down,
But your humanity pulls you up,
But limiting your personality will give you insanity,
So put the calamity of life in a box,
And show your personality like a fox,

So, whether you have short claws, long claws, sharp
claws, or no claws at all, just be yourself and show your

personality because that is who you are and limiting who
you are is limiting who God made you to be.
Show your claws and show your flaws for that is who
you are.

3 WHAT MAKES US WHO WE ARE BEAK (BELIEF)

We all have our beaks,
Our beaks are our beliefs,
Our beliefs give us relief,
Through all the pain,
We all do gain,
Some relief,
I do believe that our beliefs give us some of our Iden-
tity,
Mine is Christianity,
Others are Buddhism, Hinduism, or even Shintoism,
Believe in who you are,
What you have become,
and what you will become,
Believe in your belief,
For you will become a chief,
Though there are thieves,
That try to make you a leaf,
That floats in the air,
Be aware that this world is not fair,
It is full of questionnaires,
That try to declare you a terrifying bear,
Though I am no millionaire,
I understand you need to hold on to your belief and
your identity,
Let your beaks become meek,
So that they don´t get weak,

And let your heart speak,
Just like the ways of the Greek,
For your beak is your belief and what you believe is
what you will become.

4 WHAT MAKES US WHO WE ARE EYES (DREAMS / VISION)

We all have our eyes,
Our eyes are our dreams,
Let your dreams shine and gleam,
Make sure you fulfill your dreams,
Or you'll become a meme,
But there is always a chance to redeem,
And a chance to live extreme,
Life without dreams is a life so dark,
Life limits your bark,
So, make sure you make your mark,

Those who live big,
Already have their gig,
So, make sure you don't rig,
Your only chance to live and not constantly dig,
Fulfilling your dreams takes vision,
Some people try to bring division,
Others do subtraction,
But those who dream always bring addition
Others think their magicians,
Just because they bring demolition,
So they are scared they will get retribution,
But we should act more like pediatricians,
Because helping people should be our duty,
It brings the best in people and gives them beauty,
So, dream big,

Act big,
And be big
For our eyes give us vision and our vision make our
dreams come true

5 WHAT MAKES US WHO WE ARE FEATHERS (RACE / ETHNICITY)

They say birds of the same feather flock together,
They are one,
They act like they won,
Everywhere you go you see the sun,
Act like you're having fun,
While the others mock,
We walk the talk,
They say your feathers aren't beautiful,
We say we are beautiful,
God said turn the other cheek,
While we teach and preach,
While the finish line is in reach,
They say talk the talk,
Walk the walk,
Talk the walk,
Walk the talk,
Haters are going to hate,
Lovers are going to love,
If you hate hate you love,
If you love love you love,
If you hate love you hate,
If you love hate you hate,
There are millions of feathers,
But we are altogether,
Acting like we are all weather,

For we are all tethered together,
Practically leather
Pretending to be better than the other,
All praying abba father,
For we all have feathers,
And we are all clever
For God made us beautiful black, and white, together
we are all better together, we are clever together, we are
beautiful

6 WHAT MAKES US WHO WE ARE SONG (SOUL)

Everybody has their song inside them,
Our great song is our soul,
Without our soul we are not whole,
People try to get in control,
When they know we are on a roll,
And I feel like I´m on a stroll,
Because people try to console,
Those who have lost their soul
Your song is great,
Let us play a symphony,
For we all have our soul and our soul has a purpose
Some play their songs slowly,
Others play it quickly,
Some People play it quietly,
But others play it loudly,
But we should all play our songs proudly,
For we are great and our songs have purpose,
Our soul is just passing through,
But it will live for eternity,
While we see externally,
Our soul sees internally,

Personally, I want to live eternally,

With no anniversary,

Or remembrance of any infirmity,

I just want to live with my father who rules paternally,

He rules firmly and very earnestly,

Let our souls sing our songs

And let everybody know we are strong,

For everybody feels like they belong,

When everybody sings along,

For God was never wrong,

To put a song inside us

So let us sing,

For we do not need to lead,

But we do need to know that we have purpose and our
song will be sung for eternity.

THE STREET OF MANY COLORS

My street is full of color
dogs barking a symphony
Motorcycles rushing
Tires bursting like gunshots,
My world so full of life
filled with birds singinggggg
Bikes **buzzing,**
Booming, and Banging with ease
Balls pumping bam, bam, bam,
Kids laughing ha, ha, ha,
Babies crying Wah, Wah, Wah,
We keep living like a big family
My street so **carefree**
A sign saying **Apt.**
My house full of wonder
built on_care, chocolate, and coconuts

MY BUILDING PLAN

POEM INSPIRED BY MARTIN LUTHER KING JR. BLUEPRINT SPEECH

In my life I have built my dreams.
In my life I know my way.
Block by block I build my clay.
Story by story I build my glory.

My dreams are mine; they shine like gold.
God you are my hold in struggles old.

What is music to me?
Music is color put together for all to hear.

I am a singer, I am a pastor, I am a doctor.
I'm going to fly like a helicopter.

What is music to me?
Music is me; Music is thee; Music is plain easy.

I am a builder, my plans are mine, my plans are thine.

I am going to write my story for all to know your glory.
For all to know you are holy.

Music is mine and I am yours.

Preach, preach, preach is what I will do.
Sing, sing, sing is what I will do.
Save, save, save is what I will do.
For I am Edonusem for God has strengthened me to be me
the me he created me to be.

POEM FOR MOM

#1 POEM

To have patience,
Is to be my mom,
To be my mom you must be gracious,
From birth she has been tenacious,
To this stage she has been audacious,
Oh, my mom I am so grateful,
I am grateful for your cooking,
Grateful for your footing
Grateful for your pushing,
All because of you I know God,
I am grateful you are my mom,
Because you have patience,
The patience to find,
The patience to hide,
To abide and reside,
To know the time to choose a side,
Or the time to feel the tide,
Because of you I know God
Oh, great mom,
The one I can't choose from,
You help me stay calm,

When you hold me in your palm, or arm,
I can see the world from Vietnam to even Insawome
(Nsawam),
For because of you I know God,
Oh, mom my great friend,
The one who I can depend,
On not to extend or defend any pain,
For you recommend and intend on me to learn about
God,
For you don't pretend,
Offend, or overextend any sorrow,
For in the end,
You are my mom and you are God sent.
Mom, you give me comfort,
You put a lot of effort,
Mom you are like an instrument,
Playing your own song,
and never others,
Mom thank you,
May God bless you,
May I never forget what you
taught, may we never forget you, For because of you I
know God

2 POEM

Mom you are great,
You are a big part of my fate,
You try never to hate,
You have taught me to relate,
And try not to procrastinate,
And though it is good to live in the states,
It is hard to be a good mate,

And help others through their debates,
It is because of you I learned to be obedient.
I try not to be disobedient,
And help cook with some ingredients,
Every day you help me be resilient,
Mom you are radiant,
It is because of you I learned to be obedient,
Mom you are too bright,
You give a lot of light,
You are a great delight,
Mom you a great person,
It is because of you I learned to be obedient.
Mom, what makes you so happy?
Even though sometimes you get sentimental and sappy,
Even though your day may be crappy,
or some people make you unhappy,
You always seem to stay classy.
Though you may not be named Abby, Sammy, or
Cathay,
You are SEFAKOR and you make others and yourself
happy,
It is because of you I learned to be obedient,
Mom thank you for being you,
Thank you for being helpful,
Thank you for being great,
Thank you for the good times and the bad,
For you are my Hero,
Best friend,
Teacher,
Doctor/nurse,
Cook,
Assistant,
Mentor,

Counselor,
And most importantly my mother,
For it is because of you I learned to be obedient.

3 POEM

Mom you are not a disgrace,
You are the one I can't replace,
I feel comfort when I am in your embrace,
Mama you are the ace in every place,
It is because of you I learned to love.
Mom you are beautiful,
You are suitable,
Very dutiful,
Never delusional,
It is because of you I learned to love,
Mom you are strict in love,
You fly like a dove,
You don't even need a shove,
For you are already above,
You are loved,
You help me forgive,
It is because of you I learned to love.
Mom, you hear the voice of God,
Bringing lots of Joy,
Mama thank you for listening,
Talking and helping me understand more about God,
It is because of you I learned to love,
Mom you are not shy,
You make good pie,
I love when you say hi,
Thank you for teaching me to fly,
With wings I try,

But in education I thrive,
It is because of you I learned to love,
Mom you are a treasure,
You are a great pleasure,
A great refresher,
Mom you are very clever,
You are the center,
In every situation,
It is because of you I learned to love,
Mom, you have a wheelchair,
You don´t let it limit you,
You are like a myriagon full of many sides,
It is because of you I learned to love.

4 POEM

Mom, you try not to have any regrets,
You are not in debt,
You are not a threat,
Your melody plays a duet,
You are a great present,
You are not a brunette,
But you have dark hair,
It is because of you I learned to be kind,
Mom you are hardworking,
Mom you are not good at smirking,
But you are good at learning, serving, earning, and not
disturbing,
Mom you are not good at flirting,
It is because of you I learned to be kind.

Mom, you have a hard job,
Everybody tries to rob your light,

But around the globe,
You shine your light.
It is because of you I learned to be kind,
Mom you are warmth,
You like to perform,
Feeling like you have transformed,
Sometimes women are like storms,
Or like bombs,
They are hard to understand,
But most of the time you are like a pompom,
Very bright with colors and very fun,
It is because of you I learned to be kind,
Mom you are so funny,
You are like a bunny,
Mom you are very sunny,
You don't have a big tummy,
It is because of you I learned to be kind.
Mom, you work 24/7,
Feeling like you are the millionaire Kevin,
Even though being a mom is not a profession,
It is a great lesson,
Though the world is not heaven,
It is not hell or any other question,
Ma I am 13 but I used to be 11,
Feeling like I am a great person,
It is because Of you I learned to be kind,

5 POEM

Mom you are a role model,
You are a good Apostle,
You make good pancakes and waffles,
Mom It is because of you I learned to be brave,

Mom you always have a great clue,
I try not to stick to you like glue,
You tell me always to be true,
Our favorite color is blue,
You have a lot of self-worth and Value,
And when I am hurt you always come to my rescue,
It is because of you I learned to be brave,
Mom, we have a lot in common,
We both try to drive to perfection,
While we both have a lot of questions,
Mom you are a great companion,
And you always have a good resolution,
Mom it is because of you I learned to be brave,
Mom thank you for protecting me,
Though when I was young, I did try to flee,
It is because of that I got to see,
That you just try to protect me,
It is because of you I learned to be brave,
Mom you are fun,
You're like the sun,
You taught me to be a good son,
You always know the time to do a good pun,
It is because Of you I learned to be brave,
Mom you were once a kid,
You were never wicked,
Always seeing the good in people and having a strong
spirit,
Mom you are very passionate,
It is because of you I learned to be brave,
Mom you are from Ghana,
Where we used to see football games in an arena,
You don't like alcohol or Liquor,
You want me to become a good doctor,

It is because of you I learned to be brave.
Curiosity you are a hand that holds me tight,
Wonder you are what keeps me up at night,
Happiness is a greeting light,
And mom you kept me in my daily fight,
It is because of you I learned to be brave.

DEAR MOTHER,

You are closer than any Other,
Brighter than a sunshine summer,
You help me discover, recover, and uncover,
You are color,
Help those who suffer,
You make the best breakfast, lunch, and supper.

Mama, you are special.
You are better than any word can describe.
You have protected me from the day I was born,
I am too proud to thank you for all the good you have done for me,
Without you my life would be a wreck,
You have taught me values more important than life itself,
You're my mother who brought me from Ghana for a better life,
With this understanding I write this letter in shame for my behavior over the years.

The day I bought Candy with your money on Mother's Day when I was supposed to buy you something special,

The day I wouldn't take a picture of you on your birthday,
And even today when I asked out of impatience how many
videos I should take of you on your special day.

Mama you are the Musician of the year with your great lyri-
cal songs composed with rhythm,
Mama your food is on the front page of KTCHrebel,
Mama you are the prophetess of our family,
Mama you are the Pediatrician of the century,

Mama great momma,
You are the best in the world,
Sacrificing time for my future,
Sacrificing sleep for my health,
Sacrificing Money for my Education,

Your sacrifices do not go unnoticed great mama.

Mama you have been by my side when I fall sick and am in
pain.
Sponging late nights for my wellbeing,
Giving me lessons on basketball,
Telling me important things I need to hear about my char-
acter and personality,
You have loved me, cared for me, helped me, suffered for
my sake, cried with me, laughed with me, and you know me
more than anyone in the world.

There are stories untold of your support,
Stories untold of your kindness,
Stories untold of your love,
But one thing I know is you shall eat the fruit of your labor,
and you have impacted me in many ways than one,

Thank you for your love,
Sorry for my behavior,
Love you for all the time, money, sleep, sacrifices, kindness, support, lessons protection, and memories together.

You are the best,
The sun for our family,
Lyrics to our song,
Words in our book,
Moves in our choreography,
Strings in our guitar,
Without you our family would be incomplete and nonfunctioning.
You hold us together like superglue,

Thank you for everything and may God bless you,

Love your grateful son,
Edonusem H.A.Y. Pomeyie

MOM'S YEARS

Another day
Another Year glad to have you here,
You have been there through thick and thin.
From the womb to the world you have been the great-
est gift.
And when the times are rocky,
you know how to smooth the rough.
Every day in every way you shine your light to the
world around you.

Every year I am grateful to be your son.
The miracle,
Our miracle,
My miracle,
You are the one who's voice I listen to when I come
home.
Knowing you brighten someone else's day through the
phone.
Cause the gift you gave this year and the years you gave
before is your consistent loving voice,
Your great smile,

Your wisdom beyond understanding,
Patience for me,
The me, that sometimes doesn't make the best deci-
sions.
But I know you are there to help me find my way.
So I thank you for this year,
The 15 years,
Cause each year is your year to shine brighter,
Because each year is mom's year.
Not today,
But this year,
Because your day is 365 days,
Your day is right now,
Tomorrow,
And yesterday.
So mama happy 15 years.
For always being there.
Thank you for being my mom.

TIRED ANGER POEM BY EDONUSEM

When the silence speaks volume,
And all your anger is burning,
In the silence of your heart,
You can only laugh when the tiredness seems to grow,
Silent anger when they kill your soul.
Tired anger when you want to blow,
When all you want is happiness,
Your friends they throw,
And all you know is how to smile even if you are so low.
When I was younger,
I was diagnosed,
The good thing was I didn't fly alone,
But when you start a new life all alone,
You don't know when the tiredness will come,
And your fists do all the talking,
When you know your limit,
And the fever kicks in,
You know you are at your breaking point.
All you can do is smile,
Through all the pain,

You laugh,
And when the sun sets,
You are too tired to be angry,
And when the sun wakes from a long sleep,
You are just happy to be alive,
For your tiredness has overcome your anger.

ODE TO THE BIBLE

O Bible,
Thy words so true,
Engulfed in the spirituality of my ancestors,
Shedding light from the time the world began.

O Bible,
Do you ever grieve the lost souls in your stories,
Praise the heroes of your glory,
Or condemn the sins of our history?

O Bible always reliable,
Full of stories of trial and survival,
No other book can become a rival.

For thy colorful dreams,
intertwined in every page of writing,
Created by Apostles and prophets of the first coming,
Gleam in our minds.
O bible,
Thy leather skin and words of steal,
Can melt the souls of plenty,

And heal the wounds of many.

Thy power o word of God,
Is not known to a great deal of the multitude,
But is known to those who seek diligently.
For Thou hast our past, present, and future,
Hidden in your vast glory and holiness.

ODE TO MY PHONE

Oh phone I am sorry for my carelessness,
Sorry for my inability to stay focused in emotional situ-
ations,
I am sorry I left you trustingly in the hands of the un-
known.

Was it my excitement that caused this unthinkable,
A man so careless to leave his phone in a cubby,

Dear phone,
I wish I didn't leave you alone,
I wish I kept you home,
Phone don't leave me stone cold,
Your greatness is left in the hands of thieves,

Oh, phone, are you homesick?
I know we live in an ordinary world,
Full of twists and turns,
I still imagine you in my hands.
Photos, movies, texting... all gone.

Ode to my phone,
The phone that deserves a throne,
Oh, phone old and grown,
You helped me get in the zone,
Entertained me when I was bored and full of groans,
Thank you for being my friend.

MY TRUE BASS EDONUSEM POMEYIE

I'm a true-blue bass,
The prince ablaze,
When I sing my voice is Excalibur,
Breaking the barrier that surpasses new caliber.

My echo builds understanding,
Gives strength with capacity.
For my name is,
Edonusem Henry Pomeyie,
five feet five,
Very friendly,
A lot of people do envy,
What I carry inside.

But to know me you got to know my history,
I am full of many mysteries,
I have had many losses and victories.

Sister died at age seven,

She now lives in heaven,
Life was full of questions,
Many lessons left impressions in my soul.

Now I'm fourteen years old,
Trying to stay bold,
Heart shining like gold,
Memories bringing heavy loads,
But I always smile composed.

I'm a true-blue bass,
Blue for loyalty,
Blue for honesty,
Blue for Christianity,
Blue for strength,
For this is who I am.

DISTRACTIONS

In life there are distractions that keep us at bay,
They keep us away,
From the dreams and visions that come our way,
Our purpose and happiness can come any day,
And they may,
Be hard to achieve but we just need to say okay,
To the voice inside that will say,
Yeah, nay or hey, maybe someday,
I know my initials spell H.A.Y but life is not a hay pas-
ture,
It is hard and the distractions in life will always be
there.

So, what do you do?
You make a choice,
You make a review and find a new view,
I know that some people grew up blue,
Cause the distractions made them untrue,
And their pasts will pursue,
But you can't screw your crew,

Because they are all you have, and they help beat the
distractions.

Distractions come in different shapes and sizes,
They arise and surprise,
They are wise with lying eyes,
And their disguises imply lies,
But our prize is in the skies,
So, we cannot let the distractions stop us from finish-
ing our races,

So, keep fighting the lies,
Keep running your race,
Keep beating the distractions because they can't stop
your joy unless you let them.

PROMISED LAND

We all have a destination,
We dare to dream,
Dare to find greatness within our creation,
We dare to shine and beam

Our life has a destination,
Ours is the promised land,
A salvation,
A conclusion with a life of Grand
Wether were ready for any Precipitation,
Or the fight with contemplation,
We gotta stay strong and Stand.

Ok when there is no words left to speak,
I find that I get weak,
No just very meek,
I am trying to stay silent,
While I seek,
Find peace,
and learn to observe within the week,
Observe and dine by the creak,

This is my Promised land.

I will find my silent solace,
Within the Chaos of loud...
I will find peace even when the creek is flow less,
I'll find my promise land within my soundless,
Boundless demeanor.

For I am changing for the better,
Singing as I grow for the greater,
Never going to be left behind for the lesser,
But find strength within the blender.
The blender of life that makes me Stress her,
But I'll find Solace and soon go quiet with pleasure.

Time to be concise,
Think and speak with flow,
Its gonna take some exercise,
It's time to let them know,
Silence is golden,
And gold is what will be told,
As I speak, grow,
And never slow.

This is my promised land,
My promised land,
Promised land,
Land!

EMPATHY POEM I KNOW YOU MY FRIEND

I know you my friend,
Who looks downcast with sadness,
Like a tsunami of emotions fighting the walls of your
pupils,
Calling out to come in the form of an ocean.

Though your lips quiver on repeat,
Your hands quake with fright,
And you sniff back your frustration,
You smile at me and tell me you are all right.

I know you my friend,
Who fights lies with determination,
Asks why with contemplation,
Who tries to find the affirmation,
Through all her situation,

Though I don't know if it keeps you up at night won-
dering if someone cares,

Or you just cry yourself to sleep because that is the
only way you can,
Or you just wake up in the middle of the night because
your nightmare is too real to be fake,
And it is not a mistake that you wake up with a shake.

I know you my friend,
Who will turn your downcast to a frowned passed,
Who will turn your tsunami into an origami,
Who will shine like the sun and sing with joy of dreams
beyond.

I know you my friend,
For I was you,
Fought lies like you,
Asked why like you,
But I found peace and so will you.

I know you my friend,
Because I am your friend.

DIAMANTE POEM ABOUT EQUALITY

Equality,
Impartiality, and fairness,
Flying, liberating, running,
Forward ever, backwards never,
Separating, breaking, disconnecting,
Limited, stationary
Segregation

MONSTER POEM

Hey, my name is Bob,
And I have a good Job,
I scare till they sob,
Cause I'm a monster.

I'm green with blue eyes,
And I have a good size,
I'm tall and I'm wise,
And my laugh can surprise,
I can walk through the skies,
And even improvise.

But I'm good at what I do,
I don't need you or a crew,
I eat shoes and bamboo,
And my best friend is from a zoo,

Some Monsters think It's cool,
Others feel its taboo,
I think it's untrue and I don't believe in their point of
view.

When I was young,
I lived in the streets,
I hid from the police,
Even though I lived in Greece,
I didn't like the priests,
Cause they made me feel like I was a demon or a beast.

Now I'm famous,
I laugh more because it contagious,
I don't scare as much cause that is why the hate us,
I travel more in the sky because it is more advanta-
geous,
And the monsters think I'm courageous,
To be good.

9TH GRADE

These sets of poems were written in 9th grade. They were all written in different locations. On the Toilet, In my classrooms, On the floor of My living room, at the lunch table, On the bus. It didn't really matter. 9th grade was a time of poetic freedom for me. I was getting more comfortable writing my poetry, not just in a classroom. It was a time when poetry became a way for me to cope with my emotions. A hope outlet when I was struggling. It didn't matter the time of day, it just mattered what I had to write. In 9th grade I wrote a lot of sad poems because it was an emotional rollercoaster of a year. My freshman year, feeling a little lost in a new population, which then made me miss the comfort of my twin sister's company. Hence a Poem like "Pain Gain", which I used in my speech tournaments. Additionally 9th grade year was a time that my eyes were more open to a lot of racial injustice in society. These realizations brought on poems like "All I can say is Aah", and "How it feels to be black". These poems helped me grow more emotional in my poetry. I would call this grade my emotional poetic explosion.

ALL I CAN SAY IS AAH

(POEM ABOUT THE OPPRESSED RACE)

All I can say is Aah,
The voice and anger of our history,
All I can say is we keep running,
We keep running from the truth,
the wounds that scar so easily,
I wish that our scars from slavery,
Colonization,
would not fester,
But the angered me,
the angered history remains.
For the oppression we have faced on our own land,
For the oppression we have faced on your land,
For we have been oppressed by you,
by us,
and ourselves.
For even the past has rebelled against us.
The Minority,

always the majorly oppressed,
The minority,
always having a major chip on the shoulders cause our
past has made us angered but strong.

All I can say is Aah,
For the darkness that looms over me,
Cause the truth is a bitter pill to swallow,
The truth that we have shunned as a people...

The truth that our past has crippled our nation of
Africa,
but made the others fat on our resources.
Man, I wish it was easy to say how it made me feel,
To know,
That the fight is not over,
The fight will not be over,
The fight in our souls,
In our hearts,
In our history,
Will not be over till Africa becomes whole again, till we
regain all our lost people, resources, and history...
Africa, why is your growth paralyzed?
My homeland brainwashed through oppression,
And my people are just striving to be heard.
No,
for the truth is,
The savior mentality is in every generation,
It was the savior mentality that started colonization,
but ended in racism, sexism, colorism, all the isms of life.

I don't know if any of this makes sense,
So, all I can say is Aah,

For my oppressed self and people,
For I don't know how the future will be,
But I do hope that my Aah can resonate in every gener-
ation and change our future as a nation, as a people op-
pressed, and as an angered,
made strong.
For many have lost the truth,
Many don't know the truth,
And the truth has been silenced for generations.
Silenced the ones to bring the truth,
Like Kwame Nkrumah,
Who was imprisoned for his knowledge.
There have been many whose stories are not known,
But one day the truth will set us free from the
bondages of our past.
So let us say Aah together till our past can be remem-
bered and our futures created in a new light.

HOW IT FEELS TO BE BLACK (REVISED)

People don't know me, but they want to own me,
Frame so small I became A nine-year-old him not me,
Living life on the edge cause that's how I become the grown me,
Hoodlum cause I'm black it's in the melanin you know me,
Controlled by the voice they call whiteness,
they called free,
Name so long they got to shorten to fit them not me,
Eddie, Ed, Edon, Strength cause that's the meaning,
Chris, where the heck did Chris come from?
Just cause one day I dressed him,
I became him,
because I'm black cause I'm black all because I'm Flippin black.
You know now I understand my ancestors.
In this land they call free,
It's free for them but not free for me,
born black raised black you've just known black.
Born with so much melanin,
I became a **trespasser** at birth.

You know the question isn't if Jesus was black, the ques-
tion is did they even accept black?
cause me and my people,
my history have been the Criminals,
slaves to black, trespassers,
them people they caught with the fight in them.

What it means to be black to be raised with the fight in
    you,
called names because you're black and black is sin, right?

Heck no I'm black beauty born free but only within me ac-
cepted by no one except my family,
cause it's the black life we livin, my life, his life, and all
of the people around me. All of them around me, them
around me, around me, me, around them!

I WAS BORN A WARRIOR

I was born a warrior,
A man born with the fight within him,
Sickled at birth,
But not chiseled to death.

I was born a warrior,
Born to fight for my every breath,
Born to fight to become a Victorian,
Born to live a war within me,

I was a man born with the fight within me,
A man grown with the pains around me,
With a crisis from birth,
I was grown pained,
Me my story and I are one,
Because me I was born to die early,
Because it is a belief where I'm from that we sickled
don't live past 9,
But the Irony is me the warrior sickled had to witness
my twin chiseled to death,

Sickled at birth,
I learned the meaning to live,
In and out of hospitals that became my second home,
In and out of crisis I was raised a warrior,
I learned how to fight the battles within me because I
had to live to bring a change,
I had to live past 9 cause I was not gonna leave my mom
behind,
Because the death of a twin Ironically taught me how to
live,

Cause me I'm not chiseled to death,
I'm not chiseled to pain,
Though there are times my heart and body feel chis-
eled,
I'm not chiseled to the sickle,
I'm chiseled to change,
Chiseled to happiness,
Chiseled to God,
Chiseled to bring my story, my future, and me to the
world around me.

PAIN GAIN (WRITTEN VERSION)

Help is all that I say,
Help is the prayer I pray,
Cause day in and day out sadness is the way out,

I'm feeling chest compressed,
Distress,
ingest of pain and protest,
Oppressed by the weight of loss,
Pressed by the way of my cause,
Pain, oh what pain, help, help, this burden I feel is so
mightily felt,

Through all the pain we all do gain some relief, but what re-
lief comes through this great vast ugliness of loss,
How do you overcome that darkness that clouds, pounds,
mounds my soul to say regret,

I'm feeling chest compressed,
Distress,
ingest of pain and protest the test, the test,

Oh, what grief, to lose your twin,
No, your soul to the depths of grief,
Oh, what grief to lose your yolo lifestyle to the yoyo
lifestyle of high, no why school, sigh school, my school, so
fly school, But the days of grief days of brief, days of no re-
lief of free leaf, No belief
Sometimes I wish that nothing existed at the same time
everything existed, a paradox of sorts. My Orthodox con-
vention.
Lemonade, turn the sour to the sweet,
What if the sour is too sour to be sweet?
Does there come a point when the sourness of life kills the
sweetness of happiness?
Naturally I smile through the pain but when the stress be-
comes the oppression,
I find my way out, find my days to stand out.
So, when I become my oppression I sing that Oppression
out, When I become my stressed out, I sing that stress out.
So, life in its paradox is my comfort through the strong
box, and my comfort zone.

Comfort of life, Comfort of strife, comfort of all sorts in my
life.
When we get to a stage in life,
your comfort can be a mirage of imagination,
as a great poet once said there is no such thing as a safe
space,
So, what is my comfort?
Life in all its curiosity makes me think of who I am,
So, what makes me who I am,?
why do I sing?
Why do I try to make all the cruelty of life control my

voice?
There comes a point in time when I face my music,
I face my escape,
stop running and face my fears.
Life rhymes with strife,
Strife is hardship so in life there will be hardships,
but we must fight for our happiness.
Joy is a weapon that disarms naysayers and all the fake say-
ers.
Life to live,
to live is to find life through love,
Light,
and joy.
Have faith in humanity,
And believe that there will be a better tomorrow for hu-
manity,
The pains of life will not weigh us down.
Because together the pain turns into the brightest gain.

BLAME GAME

When something bad happens,
Who do you blame?
Come on we all do it,
Blame me, blame you, blame God, blame all,
It's called the blame game.

We all aim or frame to blame,
I do in my proclamation of shame,
Or the same in my claim of sadness that ends in flames,
Occasionally I exclaim in desperation "oh shit".
Sometimes it is a reflex to just blame names.

The people we blame,
Or the things we claim to blame,
Usually are not the causes of our pain,
Our blame games are shot but are lame since it's un-
tamed, un aimed, and full of anger,

This ballgame we usually play is useless,
Because,

The blame we make is to make others feel our pain,
But we usually drink this poison slowly thinking it will
kill the blamed,
But anger untamed is usually caused by sadness un-
solved,

So, this game we play is not to blame but to be tame,
This game we play is not to blame but to be comforted,
This game we play always ends in flames.

So, let's not blame, let's not play this game,
Let's become tame through healing, comfort, and end
in happiness.

CULTURED UNRELUCTANTLY

I just got a rude awakening,
Apparently I'm an oreo,
A white man in a black body,
Like...
What me?
The cultured me from Ghana,
Lost in this craziness of my generation.

The fact is I am a little white washed but I am not white.
The fact is I am black but not your black.
See the truth is I can't be your black.
Can't be that Man who acts all hood cause I ain't. Never
was so now just got to live my life as an oreo?

Nah cause the truth is I'm not an oreo.
I was born black raised black but not just black.
Mom never raised me to be a hoodlum.
Fact is I was raised to live a cultured life.
Truth is y'all keep talking but I am done listening to your

white noise.
All the loud noise.
I'm a Ghanaian born and raised, but also raised in a white
country.
I am a single raisin a little sugar coated.
But I am still in this white milk of this white state.
See truth is I am a little white washed, but I accept it,

Cause I am black too.
But I am not your black.
But my black.
Ghana black that made it out for my family back home to
also know that the white privilege can become the black
privilege.
That we don't have to worship whiteness to be recognized.
So yeah I am the black me cultured unreluctantly.
I went to a white private school that taught me the life of
privilege.
So I know both sides of the coin. The black side, the white
side, and the straight middle.
Furthermore I am not my father,
I am not my mother,
I am not my sister,
But I see all of them in me.
I got my fathers charm interestingly,
I got my mothers smile which makes me smile constantly,
I got my sister's voice with me,
which comforts me,
but I am not my family.
Mama always taught me to remember where I'm from,
Where I am at,
And where I'm going.
So life, me, and living,

Let's continue the journey we started remembering and
growing every chance we get.
Cause I am still getting cultured unreluctantly, but wel-
come this because I am growing through change.

THE WORD THAT KILLED

It seems all my life,
Through the thick and thin,
My mom never said the words "I am disappointed in
you" to me.
Me, the kid who used to steal peanuts from the jar with
my twin.
Me who forgot things like I had dementia.
The man who kept talking till something stupid came
out of his mouth.
<u>Disappointment is the</u> word that killed our happiness.
Disappointment: sadness, or <u>displeasure</u> caused by the
<u>nonfulfillment</u> of one's hopes or expectations.
See her whole life my mom heard the words disappoint-
ment
From her father
From the neighbors
All because she was deemed "cursed".
But the one person who never spoke those words to her
was her mom.
The word that kills all happiness was never on the lips
of my grandma.

Due to this when my mom became a mother,
she never said I am disappointed in you to her kids,
All because of the impact from that word.
She would be hurt
Turned,
Burned,
And killed by the actions of her children,
but to keep our happiness and to not destroy the hopes
and destinies of her children,
She never spoke the forbidden words.
How come through all of this the word that killed,
killed her emotionally,
mentally,
and psychologically,
all because of dreads.
The dreads that bring dread,
The historical kryptonite of every Ghanaian.
The dreads that have symbolism of flying and strength,
combination of powers I long for.
But in my haste to open Pandora's box,
To find my superpowers,
I ENDED UP STEPPING ON THE TOES OF MY CUL-
TURE.
Why is it that in my haste I pulled the trigger of the
only gun that could kill.
By speaking the forbidden words, I pulled a trigger,
Not recognizing the gun as fatal or even loaded.
I wanted dreads,
Locks,
Wings,
Strength,
Freedom,
Pleasure.

At the cost of what?

See the word that killed me was spoken by me in haste
and anger. Even though it was never spoken to me, How
could I commit such a heinous crime?
This word was used to annihilate a happy night,
The death certificate reads...
The cause of death: Disappointment
The juju spell that ruined
The gun the buried,
And the earthquake that rumbled that fateful night.

THE ME'S OF LIFE

Everyday, everyway you see that everyday smile,
Everyday, everyway you see that everyday glow,
But me, I feel like I'm changing.

The game I played,
my love... Is never staying.
When it comes to the time to shine,
I feel like I go dark.
So, when they say shine your light,
I just see yours slowly fade...
For when I was with you,
Our lights were intertwined.
Me, I'm still looking for the broken pieces.
Cause when I remember home. I can only see your
face.
Now I'm looking for your love...

Mama said you only look for love at this age if you're
trying to fill a hole in your heart.
Well now I understand.
Cause I've changed.

The young me is the same me... but now I have lost you
and felt like I lost me through you.
You see they say I'm the kindest kid in class,
but I just feel like all my glow and go has made me diss
me,
made me a diff me,
the three of me?
1. Happy me, the kid who shines his light through his
happiness,
2. The sad me, the part that longs to see your face
through the smile of the sun.
3. The love me... the guy who loves to be loved by her,
the girl who doesn't know that she is my peace.
4. The forgotten me.
The one who pretends everything is as was,
to the point where the forgotten me becomes the got
me the forget this me...
the me that cries knowing his twin will _never_ tell him
goodnight, as their all-night late conversations turn a
night into morning daylight.
You know why I forget things lately?
It's because the forgotten me starts to forget the world
exists because he has already created his own.
They call it dellulu. I, myself, and I call it Utopia.
Edomdedzi did you know I laughed when they said
you died?
It was funny because you aren't dead.
My twin, my nurse apprentice help, my friend.
The one who tells me to remember my table manners...
you can't be dead.
You must live to continue to tell me to remember my
table manners.

Sometimes in my utopia I expect you to rise from the
dead,
but you've been gone for 8 years now! When will I stop
thinking of the girl who first broke my heart...

Truth be told,
This is not poetry.
This is a tragedy.
Cause the bleeding of my soul has cut through the
bleeding of pain.
The longing for peace has cut through my memories.
I'm too young to die insane.
But the pounding of my memories of pain has caused
the shine to fade.
It may be due to my more play than pray, but GOD
knows that my sins aren't my end.
Because Edonusem does not mean strength anymore it
means forsaken to learn through pain.
Strength,
I wish it came so easy,
My body looks weak,
but the spirit is not broken yet.
I've changed.
The young me has grown up to understand that smiles
are the fronts on every battle inside.
The smile is your comfort.
My smile is my comfort and strength so I will be strong
though my memories may bash me.
I'll live for your memory to live on inside me.
especially in everything that I do.

EXPLANATION OF THE FORGOTTEN ME:

the forgotten me is forgotten to the point that it was forgotten to be written. The three of me? The fourth me is the forgotten me which I forgot to write on purpose. I try to forget that forgotten me even though it is there as that fourth me in the Me's of Life.

THE DAYS OF PAIN

It always starts with a kind of breaking,
A kind of Tug of war,
Whether it be mentally,
Whether it be Physically,
Whether it be spiritually,
It always starts with a break.

For me my days of Pain,
I didn't see any gain,
For my days of Pain,
I saw a lot of rain,
I just couldn't refrain,
Or try to retain,
Cause everytime my breaking
Was brought on by my heart aching,
I was aching for a kind of Validation that kept me tak-
ing,
Making, and staking, everything for mistakes that al-
most kept me raking.

Raking, raking, raking, and chasing the impossible.

My days of Pain started spiritually,
I kept blaming the source of my strength repeatedly,
Kept blaming myself painstakingly,
Kept looking, kept seeking, and searching for the blame
of her death, not knowing that would leave me out of
breath,
And it left my health,
With no stealth,
my spiritual wealth,
with no breath,
Give me strength,
Give me strength,
Give me the Strength I long for.
That kind of prayer brings challenges that you fight
with strength.
Give me breakthrough,
Give me breakthrough,
Give me breakthrough,
That kind of prayer opens doors that help you discover
your true self.

You see my days of pain started spiritually,
And now I'm overthinking literally,
Lost myself mentally,
Thinking too seriously,
And falling too quickly.
Falling for the same lies these girls be saying,
You were the first to say I love you,
But the last to mean it when I'm with you.

but its aight though,
Cause Mentally I'm scarred,

Spiritually I'm no longer on guard,
And now emotionally I'm insane.
Feeling like I lost my way,
Feeling like it everyday,
Feeling like it even in the month of May,
Feeling like I don't even gotta say.
Cause I've been lost,
At what cost?
At the cost of my heartache,
Heart break.

Lastly, physically...
I've been fighting my demons,
Been fighting for so many reasons,
Been fighting in every season,
Been fighting the pain,
been fighting through the rain,
Cause I threw up yesterday,
Feeling better today,
And yet the pains of my physicality,
Not respecting or claiming my name basically,
And making me scream repeatedly.
Caused so much pain.
Cause my name means God has strengthened me yet
my body is so weak,
And I know this makes me meek,
But I hate being..
Hate being,
Hate being the voice that can't speak,
That can't peak
I hate being in one spot just cause I can't breath
through these wheezing beaks.
Cause I did seek,

Dreamed too far,
Dreamed too far about a game I can't play.

Now I'm sad,
cause I played for way too long,
But cause I don't got the stamina,
I be playing too wrong,
Thinking I be playing like king Kong,
Is it time I hit the gong?
Maybe I should stop playing...
Cause I play like I just hit the bong,
Cause I'm out of breath,
Looking at death,
And I ain't even ran for long.

Cause physically I'm sickled,
Im asthmatic,
And cause of that I'm practically crippled,
Yet I run,
Run for what?
Run for you?
Run from you?
I run to the memories?
Or run because it's death's stories.
Most people don't know me.
Most people think they flow with me,
But sadly I'm experiencing my days of pain,
Don't know when I'm gonna find the gain.
But low key forgetting I'm living in the rain.
And no one can retain,
Or regain,
The days that pass too quickly.

MEMORIES POEM

Memories,
Your memories,
Trying to let them fade,
Never let them break,
No decay,
Thought over time that only good memories stay,
Nah but it's the ones that hurt,
The ones that try to burst,
Through the day, in every way, every May. Nah cause it's the month of May, the month of September, the month I remember, every month even in December.
Cause I'm trying to forget the blue in your face,
The pink in your face, nah the sink of sadness of tears unheard.
Yeah cause you were born in September,
Our September.
Dead in April,
even using Advil never helped.
Cause the pain ain't physical.
Buried in May,
trying to forget the black coffin you rest in.

Buried in May trying not to remember everyday.
Cause you died twin.
Died,
Left me to win,
Left me to try not to sin,
Left me to never be pinned by the memories,
Your memories,
Our memories.
Cause there are some memories we hope fade, we hope
never happened, but it seems those memories never fade.
Let the memories go, no let them help you grow, try not
to explode, cause you are still living, still breathing,
So...
Memories,
Your memories,
Trying to let them fade,
Never let them break,
No decay,
Thought over time that only good memories stay,
But I'm gonna let the bad ones help me grow.
Help me go,
Help me to flow,
Help me, help me, not to blow.

GRATITUDE POEM

Gratitude,
Thanking you in the times of aptitude, or even in atti-
tude.
Your kindness and help over the years are immeasur-
able.
Thanks, is a word that we all say but sometimes taken
for granted so this is why we say it, why we appreciate it,
the characteristics of a person to be thankful for...
T- thoughtful
H-helpful
A-angelic/ amiable
N- nurturing
K-kind
S-sweet

We thank you for these qualities over the years.
Gratitude in every altitude,
in every latitude and longitude,
You are a great example of beatitudes.
For in every step of the way you have been there for us,
A family together building each other up,

You are a father, leader of a family brought together by
your generosity.

Gratitude is gratefulness with a positive attitude,
Our gratitude is too great to express, but this is my gift
to you,
Words that appreciate all you have done. So, from me
to you,
Akpe, Gracias, Merci, thank you, in all the languages I
know.
You are one of a kind.

HAHA CONFUSION POEM

I am officially confuzzled,
Confused,
Puzzled,
To no end.

I write my poetry,
Write my choreography of words,
My lyriciology,
In my symphony.

Poetically getting my justice,
I know it takes practice,
Finding peace even through all the...
Yeah you never know
I'm overthinking again,
Cause she ignores,
I just re-instore,
Find my voice within my core,

I try my best in this world,
I just want to live without a care in the world,

But I just laugh away my confusion,
Trying to create a fusion within my solution,
But my equation is not adding up in this subtraction...

A magician is only as good as his act,
But I just react,
In this world where in fact,
All I can do is react,
As I recontact.
My feelings in a world blinding the seeable,
The reachable, the feasible.

I scream,
I hear my music within my soul,
But no one hears me.

I'm confused,
This awkwardness,
I die I rise,
I fight and here we are,
Fighting
Re visiting ,

I'm confused,
Overstimulated,
Life never estimated,
Yeah I'm confused by the feeling in my chest.
Perplexed by the longing for acceptance.
For completeness,

Respect,
What is the inspection of my heart that begs for love?
Im blanking,

Re tanking
Re spiralling in this feeling of hate.
But yet to find a mate... in the confusion of a past,
Wish it was the last,
But my hate is for those I love.

Love,
Never recover,
Cause it is just a buffer,
I must forget her,
Cause she'll just break me,
Just gonna take me,
Forget me and shake me.
I keep it fake,
Cause if I don't it'll just wake me.

A ship lost at sea,
But laughing my confusion away.
Not caring about any fee,
Cause I'll always just say,
Love is not for me.

So here we are,
Laughing hysterically,
Frontin with all our hearts,
Cause we know if we don't laugh,
We'll cry,
Or end up doing something worse,
Like fly...fly in our heads to the point where we wish
our delusion was our only solution.
So I'll laugh,
Cause I haha my way out of confusion.

F-R-I-E-N-D-S

Friends as in _forever?
Friends as in _really not in love?
Friends as in _interested in you but don't want to end
this friendship?
Friends as in "entrusting you with my deepest secrets
but don't tell anyone" ?
Friends as in _never do that again?
Friends, as in _do you like anyone knowing that I only
like you?
Friends as in _so tight we are as close as siblings?

Friendship with a girl is complicated,
You love,
You don't love,
You wish you kissed,
But do you?
Is this love?
A song created over time not by one person but by a
generation used to... being different, used to fighting
boundaries, used to trying to find their place. Me, I am too
young to fully understand love... But with the complica-

tions of knowing you and knowing her, it's so hard to stay in the Zone. the red, the box, the mountain you see but never can overtake. We all know it... the friend Zone. In other words, <u>the door of no return.</u> There are friends and there are F-R-I-E-N-D-S.

Sometimes we want more, but do they?

Then the weird feelings start to form.

You smile more around them, you can't help but notice every little thing they do like how their eyes flutter when they are tired, or the way they giggle when they are nervous. Well true friends will notice these things, right? But the ultimate indicator is your heartbeat...

The boom boom, goes bang bang bong de bang, zoom zam, swoosh, ahhh. And you end up with that nervous fluster. Are we still friends?

Now why do I keep thinking of her?

She is just my friend. Get that into your thick brain. But... but she looks... beautifully amazing, pause...what am I saying? Do I like her??? But we are just friends. She will never like me like that, right? There comes a point in time when some friends become F-R-I-E-N-D-S, but love is friendship. Love is complicated like that; love is breaking down the boundaries. Love, Love, Love makes friends. So, no matter if you want to be friends or more just be honest, with you, God, Life, and her. Be true to love. I sometimes wish I could fully understand and describe love, but I realize love is love. Indiscriminately indescribable. It is you, the world, and I in a nutshell. Love gives friendships, builds them... or breaks them and makes them stronger. Don't be afraid to love, love. I learned love doesn't say love, it shows love.

So, friends or no friends love your love whatever type you have.

STARTED WITH A HEY

It started with a hey,
My love for you,
Every time you smile a little angel sings a while,
Every time you laugh the sun shines on the Nile,
I know when you giggle the clouds stop and runs a mile,
Because you are the most beautiful,
Kindest,
Most genuine,
Most, most,
Incredible,
Talented,
Sincere girl I have ever met,
I dare say the girl of my dreams.

Ok
Now I am 15, mom thinks that my love for you is all
about your beauty,
But me... you make me want to cry and laugh at the
same time; you make me happy without even trying. Your
voice is a song that takes all the emotions in my life and
turns them into unforgettable unconditional uncontrol-

lable drugs. Paralyzing pain killers that put you in a state
of confusion is my definition of love.

Love is a blessing and a curse,
A poison and a cure,
Love, love oh how to explain how I feel,
Dang the way you do your thing I can't help but smile,
Even when I see your reflection it makes me... Sing.
Oh, to see you, oh to hear you, oh to explain, to refrain,
reclaim how my feelings for you make me... sing.
Sing on the top of my lungs, sing all your pains away,
Sing our pains away.

For love though it can't be explained,
Heals our scars, heals our past, heals the pain, the
trauma, for we all need love to stay loved.

It all started with a hey,
The shot of this bullet,
Poisoned arrow that makes me feel...,
Unpained, untrained, released, retreat, fly or fight for
this feeling we call love.

Love does exist.
What?
Love?

Love... L-O-V-E,
L- Laugh, live, leap together,
O- Overcome, overtake, challenges together,
V- value, Validate, vocalize, vindicate each other with
your actions,

E- Entrust, encircle, explain, exclaim each other with
openhearted conversations,

Love is an experience shared together, once one sided
becomes Logo,
Solo
LoLo
Love.
Because you fly solo, you feel so Low you go so Low you
get a solo, logo, lolo love... The love so many people expe-
rience.

But I'm built differently.
Even if cupid won't shoot his dart, I will shoot mine,
Till my solo love becomes Our love. Shared together, we
laugh, cry, smile, sing, yell, yap, together, because love is
an emotion indescribable except for laughing... Crying, ba-
sically all the emotions into one.

Started with a hey,
Ended with you might be mine one day.
I might be okay.
ended with a, ended with a... a way?

LOVE POEM

What is love?
Love is both sweet yet painful,
Incredible yet awful.
So, what happens when the Incredible meets the awful,
the sweet meets the painful?

Love happens.
Love is Passion,
full of glory and Compassion.
Love is a cannon,
If let stocked in a cabin,
Without being blown, it will blow everything.

Cause our emotions can become ticking bombs,
If not taken care of it will become a nuclear bomb,
If not protected, yet released it becomes a vulnerable
bomb,

The most dangerous bomb is the love bomb,
It puts you in a state of ecstasy,
But once broken,

It could put you in a state of a restless sea.
Love should be our destiny,
But it's complexity,
Puts us in a state of perplexity.

To fall in love is a great thing.
To fall out of love is a learning process.
To have your heart broken is a painful thing.
But to experience all of love is to be rich.

LIVE POEM

The act of living is great.
To be living in this great world is bittersweet,
Humanity in all its <u>glory</u>,
Has shaded what it truly means to live.

To live is to give,
Forgive, relive, and believe the unthinkable,

My mother taught me to live with love,
Live with the greatness above,
Live with the understanding that one day I will go to
the world above,
And receive in love the greatness of my creator.

You know My family is centered in the belief that God
will return one day,
Does that mean that our lives should not be lived?
People fear the end, which is death,
But we should be more afraid of not living, when we are
still on this earth.

You may ask, what does he mean?
I mean that our life should be a living testimony of his
greatness.

Because Life in all its <u>glory,</u>
Is Gods,
and our God lives.

LIFE POEM

Life such an abstract word,
Life gives and takes,
Life is God in us, the hope of <u>glory.</u>

I wonder How it would be like if we could see life before
life,
Life before death,
And Life after death?

How would this great movie begin or end,
Or would it even have an end?

You know the moments in your life when you feel like
you lived through this before?
When you feel like it's a De Ja Vu moment?

It is because De Ja Vu means already seen,
and it has by God, but the moment you realize is the
moment God wants you to know the outcome, or the out-
come that could be of that instance in your life.

So, when you have that De Ja vu moment don't be sur-
prised.
Because God has already seen and wants you to be in
on his secret.

To have life there must be death...
The experience of death is not bad...
Because would there be living if there was no dying?
Life gives us an opportunity to live before our time on
this earth passes away.
So let us always remember that eternal life is in God.

10TH GRADE

This year was a year of growth in my poetry. I stopped relying on Rhyme Zones for my poetry. I started writing from my emotions more clearly. This poetic year helped me grow and come to terms with some struggles within me. During times like this I wrote poems like "The Change", the "Rights of the Knights", and more. I wrote these poems everywhere and started to perform my poems everywhere. At tournaments, during school Assemblies, and in classrooms. Poetry became a language I spoke and wrote in. It became life. So I would call this year my Poetic growth year, because I learned to fly solo with my poetry and let the words flow through me.

MY PEOPLE

They say My People were cunning,
They say my People were fighters,
They fought against their captivity,

Cause they calculated their escape,
Thought of their way of going forward while going
backwards.

Cause the legend goes my people were slaves,
They didn't live in caves,
They were surrounded by their own wall of Jericho,
But their wisdom brought them their saves,

Cause they plotted against our Oppressor in Egypt,
Gave him the party of his life,
While we peed,
We spit,
And got freed.
Cause our Oppressor was rich,
Our oppressor was a stitch,
But my people never snitched

Never snitched our plans of escape,
Just gave the big back black,
His meat,
Just gave him his feast,
And let him eat.
Cause while he ate, we were no longer bait,
While he ate, we ran before he could forget his taste,
And while he ate, we walked backwards stepping in
each other's footsteps in a single file mile.
Miles miles miles,
In sand and in grass,
Thanking God for our genius,
Thanking God for Math.

We calculated by mathematical genius,
Calculated every gallon of water we drank,
Till we freed ourselves from our Jericho.
Our Oppressor didn't see it coming,
While he fed,
We fled,
While he fed,
We fled
We fled across Egypt,
Fled across Africa,
Finding our way home,
To Togo,
To Benin,
To Ghana,
To Nigeria
and till this day...
Our single footstep,
Guides the Ewe people back home.
Back to their Genius,

And back to our freedom.

MY PEOPLE (THE ACTUAL LEGEND)

The legend goes that the Ewe people were slaves to an Evil Egyptian man. This man owned thousands of slaves and he made a compound wall around them making it too tall and too thick to escape. But the Ewe tribe calculated how much water they drank, calculated how often they would pee, and their population. They calculated all this and figured out that if any time they peed on the wall and spit on it the chemical would make the wall that they were surrounded with crumble slowly. So they waited and on the faithful night that they calculated the wall would crumble they were ready to flee. But they first created a feast for the Egyptian slave owner, and while he ate, they walked for miles going backwards stepping in each other's footsteps so it seemed only 1 person came into the compound. Even though thousands fled that night finding their new homes in the countries they settled in.

THE RIGHTS OF THE KNIGHTS POEM

They ask me, "Do you believe you can fly?"
I told them "way up in that sky?"
Me, I Believe I Can Fly...

but maybe not so high.
cuz sometimes I just can't help but sigh.
cuz in my life sometimes I just find that in my eyes
there are some lies
lies of one who is not yet accepted,
who has not yet accepted,
that he is different,

The life of a poet living in the shadows,
yet living in the light...
my story to be told,
or Untold,
My story is still yet to unfold,
My story is my hold in a world full of hate and sorrow.
I follow, I follow, I follow!

No, never borrow.
but this is my life my light,
But sometimes there is a hollow,
hmmm what a sorrow,,,
But do you follow?

Do you follow your flight for happiness?
In this sense where do you find your rights?
Come to think of it, are you right?

no cuz I am just coming to this acceptance of rights of
the lights,
Right not of the of the nights,
It's not so black and white,
because the light of the whites always has the rights...
but the rights of the knights in the night are left in
darkness.

My people have never had the rights!
Aw it's coming to me, the rights of the lights... Yes,
what a grand plan.
they have dictated our rights they thought were right
for the dark knights,
Dictated our lights way from the beginning.
And yet here we stand such strong knights of the
night.
Still standing fighting for our rights fighting to be
heard through this darkness of the night.

As you sleep and wake,
As you sleep and wake,
Thinking of a grand plan,
thinking of a grand plan of a life you wish could be...

They ask me, "Do you believe you can fly?"
I told them "way up in that sky?"
Me, I Believe I Can Fly...
yes me I Can Fly,
right through the sky,

I am a black star,
a star that is shining even when the light might scar.
Yes, me I Can Fly,
I will fly till this knight finds his rights,
yes, even in the darkness of the nights.
Yes, I will fly so that this night will become light even-
tually.

TO RELATE IS TO CREATE POEM

To relate is to create
To create is to be great,
When you relate, our world becomes a mighty state.

To relate is to create,
Create from the relationships that teach you,
Teach you to be you,
Teach you to create from two,
Teach you to create for me and you
Teach you to find the sanity in the relationships you create.

To relate is to create,
For when tragedy strikes it is our ability to relate that creates change,
The changes we create all relate to our understanding of ourselves and community.
For change is great when you change for two, change for you, change for me and you.

For we relate as a nation but not as a single story,
We relate to the unity in all of us that tells us that to-
gether we stand, but divided we fall.

To relate is to create,
For I am a creation of two not of 1,
A combination of of genes from mom and pop,
A creation that we all know to be true
When two or more are gathered I'm in your midst,
The creation of two is where we see the spirituality of
you,

To relate is to create,
For I learned my greatest lesson when I learned from
my greatest loss,
You see twins know the value of two,
To relate on a level no one understands.
You see when you lose a twin that the value of two be-
comes a value of one.
When you lose your half you are reborn in a raft.
A raft that teaches you the greatest lesson you could
ever have.
The lesson to create as we relate to one another and to
ourselves.

THE GUN POEM

I decimate,
And reinstate,
I turn you into bait,
I demolish your estate,
I decide your fate

I live in a world where I choose who lives or dies,
I'm no God but in this world I can act like one,
Created to kill, I only have one purpose,
The laws of the jungle kill or be killed is the game I cre-
ate,
I say boom and you're gone, I say click boom and
there's no way you're speaking,
Never miss,
Never doubt my strength
Cause in a blink,
you could be dead,
In war I'm the ultimate secret weapon,
On the streets I'm the terrifier
Gangs know my rule,
But no one can control me.

I did not choose my destiny,
But you do,
You either pull the trigger and release my chaos,
But I decide how dead you are,

Death...
Death is my body,
And life is my power,
The more I claim.
The less you gain.
I've caused many funeral songs,
But it's not my fault I can't choose my destiny,
It's all yours.
Your fault I scare,
Your fault I flare,
Your fault I dont care,
Who lives is rare,
When my shot rings,
You better take your pair,
Run like you got no... bang

WEED PERFUME POEM

I walked down the street today feeling down,
Feeling like I was about to drown,
But then I got a whiff of perfume,
And a twinge of weed..

Sometimes in my life I feel like I'm drowning,
Trying to stay afloat,
But all this life is intoxicating...
Weed too strong for me to breath,
Breath, breath, breath...

Is it just me?
Or do you also smell it when I'm with thee?
But we Just can't see,
See, see, through all this foggy mess?
This truly is a sea...

We live life surrounded by this foggy weed scent
Living,
Breathing,
Inhaling,

Intoxicating,
regurgitating life.

Life we lived thinking we would just be smelling roses.
With different poses... guns blazing,
Running,
gunning for that finished line haven.

Heaven right?
Heaven...I miss thee up there in the blue skied haven,
Twins song,
Our bond so strong It is a never ending perfume.
I still see you like a mirage,
Still smell you like a passing breeze...
A teasing feeling letting me know I'm here all alone.

Life's weed is not what I'll feed,
I'll feed my positivity with creativity.
Build Up my curiosity like I'm discovering gravity,
And enjoy life to a point where I consume negativity
and spit out generosity. I'll be my own perfume in a world
of intoxicating weed.

I walked down the street today feeling like it was going
to be a great day,
I wished that feeling would stay,
But the day likes to play,
And never stays the same.

By the end of the day,
My happiness went away,
And was soon replaced with the scent of weed...

The only thing that kept me doing good deeds were the words of perfume my friends and family said to me... What is a symphony? A harmony of smells that create a tapestry. A tapestry made so relentlessly it was shown with grace.

PRESSURE POINT POEM

When your heart starts beating,
Starts pumping,
You start fleeing,
Even Fleeting,
Maybe imagining,
Just know its pressure,
Maybe Asthma.

When you stop breathing,
You start sweating,
Fastly pacing,
Never staying,
Just know its pressure,
Maybe Asthma.

I was never really good with pressure,
Always hated the temperature,
Yeah the feeling of sweat even during the cold weather,
Yeah, never was good under pressure.

I hate the phrase be the better man.

It doesn't take into account the fact that to be better,
you have to know better.
Even if you know better,
Would it be accepted with happiness like a floating
feather?
I hate the pressure that phrase puts on you.
Yeah they ask me who are you?
Who are you to just be you?
You can never do you.
Because giving you power in life makes us feel like doo
doo,
That's how I picture the white man's perspective of a
black man's respective,
prolly expressive,
even deceptive,
Perspective

I'm in control of my own destiny...
but a white man's opinion can decide my residency,
Guess that's why they call it presidency.
But Now I understand my black brother's hesitancy,
In a society made by them but never for them.

To be the better man in a society of worser men would
ostracize you like a leather can.

How could I be better when the leaders don't lead me
better?
Feed me better...
With wisdom,
So, I can build my own kingdom.

Who's to teach me better in a society of flaws?

A society I live in with my claws,
A society I feel so much pressure in I hear my heart
beat so raw.

I'm one man.
They say be the change you wish to see,
They say be the light in the darkest sea,
They say do right for you to grow like a tree,

Honestly I'm tired of being the better man,
Tired of being the light they try to ban,
Tired of doing right but reciprocated with a frying pan,

It just keeps hitting my pressure point,
I've reached my boiling point,
I'm tired of carrying around this pain in my joint.

So, I'm turning to the night,
Because fighting is not right,
My sight is caught with such blight,
Never really understood what they meant by light.

So now let my right be on my own terms.
And I'll do my own perms,
For my own benefit.

THE DAY I DIE POEM BY: EDONUSEM POMEYIE

The day I die,
The day I die let the world know,
The day I die let the world know I lived,
The day I die let the world know I lived despite the fact
it didn't want me.
From Kings,
To slaves,
A colonized nation,
To a segregated population,
A disrespected generation....
Living in a society,
Not accepting me.

I've learned to Embrace my misery,
And turn it into my victory,
Have a positive spin,
On the negative within.

How Can I see?

How can it be?
My history...
Is part of my mystery.
This is what I see.

For there to be peace,
There must be some ease,
But my life will just crease...

I go through life hoping to be somebody,
But my history...
It disturbs me!
This society...
Confuses and surprises me.
Feeling ostracized and alienated...
This is my story.

Will I get to my destiny?
Maybe eventually?
I see deeply,
As I find my voice in this tapestry,
My destiny is my destination.
Yet my hesitation...
is not my own but of this nation...
Will they accept me after segregation?

My greatest fear is death.
I'm afraid to die and leave no memory,
To be one in many who lost their dignity,

I'm afraid of my story...
My story...
Story I say repeatedly,

Hoping my story does not cause disharmony,
Cause my story is its own melody,
And their voices create their harmony.
Their own harmony,
Dragging me down,
While I drown,
Trying to find my own melody,
My independence,
In this residence.

It sucks that they want me to be a slave,
But I'm going to be brave,
Always searching for what I crave,
I'm not going to be stuck in their cave.
That they save...
But never for me.

A microaggression I've faced my whole life.
Fighting the mosquito bites that take my soul,
I'm just tired.

Faced the same quotes daily...
That I just get so lazy,
Even getting complacently crazy.
They would rather have an enemy,
Become so friendly,
And forget their own brothers and sisters.

The day I die,
The day I die let the world know,
The day I die let the world know I lived,

The day I die let the world know I lived despite the fact
it didn't want me.
For I did survive,
Did not congregate to connive,
I did survive,
Despite all the hate,
Despite the bites...
That don't revive,
I did survive,
I did survive,
I did survive.

THE CHANGE

We came home scurrying like beavers,
Then the change came,
It started with a fever,
Still she played games,
Not minding the fact that she was hot,
Not minding the fact that she was hot,
Not minding the fact that she was not,
Okay...
Mama said, "Girl go take a shower, you too hot for my
liking"
Little did we know that her shower would leave us
wishing.
Cause it took 3 days.
Our bags splayed out for the journey we were about to
take.
My sister's Cinderella doll still unopened on her Ghana
must go... looking like a princess flake.
Never knowing she was not gonna take,
And that her hair would never make
And that she would never bake.

It took 3 days
Wednesday, Thursday, Friday while we were going on
that Monday.
But death waits for no one...
Death waits for no one...
And that's how death won.

You see, what we expect is not always what always hap-
pens.
I was the sick one,
Not the picked one,
So how did she die instead of me?

Seeing death is funny.
It likes to play games.
So funny that while I slept soundly on that 3rd day,
The blue faced monster went away,
Cause while I slept soundly on that 3rd day,
My sister flew away.
My twin was the chosen 1,
Or so I thought,
So how did she die 3 days before we were supposed to
go to America
How could she leave that princess unopened in her
antarctica,
I was told recently that Poetry is my life,
And singing is my wife,
And that I should have more personality to me than
that,
But my poetry is my mystery
And my singing is my victory,
How could I say no to the only way I can say hi to my
sister.

Cause the last time I saw my sister smile,
She was dressed in blue,
The last time I saw my sister alive her face was blue,
And the other times I see her is on the stage spotlight
blue,
So blue is her mystery,
And red is my victory...
SO we are flame and water creating air...
The air that lifts to the heavens filled with care,
And the air that calms me when I flare.

Death is funny,
So funny I laughed so hard at my Uncle's Joke.
Your sister is dead...
I laughed cause how could she when I slept so soundly?

The death that comes and leaves your sister suspended
like that Cinderella doll still unopened...
It's funny because you wish it was a joke but it's not.
Was it coincidental that she died 3 days before Amer-
ica,
Was it coincidental that all she was, was blue,
Was it coincidental that I used to love blue,

Is it Coincidental that I am still alive wishing to sing 1
more time with you.
Is it coincidental that your name means God lifts you
high,
Is it Coincidental that... I wish I...saw you one last time.

Cause I slept so soundly,
And you sleep eternally,
And I miss you perpetually,

And you sing repeatedly,
On that blue stage,
With red lighting
Wearing white,
And singing with me eventually.

Cause the change came,
And my anger still aflame,
Still I'm not the same,
But your light still makes me feel sane.
And though there's rain,
And though there's pain,
Your light will always remind me never to forget the
gain.

SYMPHONY OF COMMOTION POEM

I highlight my path,
And try to lead with no wrath,
I know my place is not always right.
But I just wish my light would never be darkened by the
night.

In this world I play my symphony,
It is full of commotion,
But with all these emotions,
I create an ocean.
Yes I vote for this motion.
That life would get its own manual or potion.
But all I have is a lot of questions and a bottle of lo-
tion...
For my melanated skin in this white dessert.

I play a symphony...
Full of melody,
No harmony

because I'm just a solo act.
Yes I have instruments,
but like a banjo in a horn section, I usually feel out of
place.
I smile big... with no sorrowed trace,
But inside my heart is a troubled face.

I wish to find my voice in this hallowed race,
But bit by bit,
I hit a chord with perfect commotion,
A commotion within my ocean,
The ocean of my soul that beckons this notion.

For I play a symphony,
A solo act of melody,
A symphony of symmetry,
That I find exquisitely lonely.

I'm exactly what you call a poker-faced faker.
Because within this symphony,
There is disharmony,
Never showed this dishonesty,
Just smiled with so much bravery,

Back when I was ten,
I was feeling so free,
The big one Zero,
Feeling like I just scored a three,
Didn't need a watch like Ben,
Just needed my voice to become my own hero,
Back when I was ten,
I felt like a young man among men...

Now my symphony blares chaotically,
Blares yet so melodiously,
But I'm feeling so caged...
Feeling so brazed,
So crazed!

Do you want to talk about your feelings?
Do you want to talk about your heart,
Let me tell you how I see it.
It takes more just to believe it,
But living life far apart,
I can see much more than your Start,
I see your heart,
Your start,
Your art
inside your cart.

Now do you see me?
As I see thee,
Do you see my heart?
Or does my bravery,
Deceive thee,
Just as it deceived me.

This bravery,
Resulting in its hypocrisy,
Actually, does deserve an award for its delivery,
For its deceit is so Imperfectly perfect.
I look sane...
Though I feel the pain,
I cover it up with so much bravery,
that it starts to incinerate me.

My bravery in this chaotic symphony is a mask.
It's almost a task,
Don't let them in...
It will result in a sin,
For I just pin,
All my misery on my kin.

But as I am brave,
I do crave,
I crave to behave,
I crave to save,
For my melody is created with conductors who help
lead,
Who help feed,
And help me to see...
That my bravery is more than a mask,
It is what makes me ask...
Are we friends?
YES?
OF COURSE!
WE ARE BROTHERS!
So within this symphony there are those who make it
an orchestra of immense music.

THE STRONG STAY SOLID (NAME POEM)

Everytime I cry,
Everytime I try,
Every time I talk,
Every time I walk,
My name is the wings that carry me to fly.

In my culture names are your badge of honor,
But sometimes mine feels like a crime.
I was named from a verse my mom found in her medi-
tation.
I was named with such greatness that sometimes it's
easier to hide.
I know some people wish they had a different name but
me,
My name is the reason I'm alive.
Cause the day I was born the clock started
The times that even the devil thought I died,
My name brought me out alive.

But I'm sad,
I'm sad that my song was not lifted high,
That her name meant God lifted her high,
So high that even when I look at the sky...
I can only see the clouds waving goodbye

Cause my name gave me power,
But with great power comes great challenges.
Everytime I try to say something,
So much trauma,
Everytime I try to create something,
So much drama.

Edonusem Is my name,
And ball is my game,
Singing is my claim to fame,
And pain is what I tame,
Everyday I sing with so much vibrato I break the
frames.

Edonusem is the name,
Hedonism is the crazy take,
Cause my name is so special it always autocorrects to
Hedonism.
Google don't know me yet,
But you are looking at the dream deferred,
Dream deferred so deferred it got referred to create
greatness.
Sometimes my name feels like a crime,
Cause people are so scared to say it,
Like if they do...
the grounds would fall,
People look at me expecting me to say it,

cause they don't want to butcher my history.
But my history can't be butchered.
Only when you stay silent does my name not give you
strength.

I dream with my name,
I dream for J.E.S.E.F
J-Jesus,
E- Edomdedzie
S- Sefakor
E- Edonusem
F- Family,

And my dreams are my names

For Edonusem is my name and it makes me strong,
For Henry is my name and it makes me Colonized,
For Atsu is my name and it makes me a twin,
For my name is Yao and it makes me Thursday,

And Pomeyie is our name... and it makes us holy axes.
Cause it could be a family of holiness or a family of
jaggedness,
Lost so much that our names could cut you senseless.
Cause Pomeyie means holiness but it also means axes.
The axes that burst with history and cuts with mystery,
The axes filled with holiness and sharpened with glori-
ness.
But holiness is an ax of its own.
It cuts through the guilt of sadness.
And build with the voices of happiness.

So I am a holy ax,

Cutting down the doubts that bought me,
Cutting down the curses that try to take me,
And cutting down the pains of my past.

I was born abstract,
So abstract that there's none but me,
Even in the Ewe names I am the only Edonusem In the
whole world,

We were born abstract,
So excited to live we came out 2 months early,
So abstract we fought to live everyday,
In and out of the hospital we thought that I had been
chiseled to death,
But my name... Let me live once more.

Names,
the meds that make you flare,
or flame with care
It is my name that brought me out of darkness.
And my name that made me fly.

Cause the strong stay solid,
Time I stay stoic,
Time I stay strong.
For I am Edonusem, made to stay strong.

Extra backstory of my name

My twin and I were named from the bible verses Psalm
28 verse 7-8, and Psalm 92 verse 10. My mom during her
pregnancy stumbled upon this verse and created it, origi-

nally combining the two verses which she read in Ewe to
come up with the summary of God has strengthened me
and lifted me high.
Psalm 28 verse 7-8
The Lord is my strength and my shield;
my heart trusts in him, and he helps me.
My heart leaps for joy,
and with my song I praise him.

8
The Lord is the strength of his people,
a fortress of salvation for his anointed one
Psalm 92 verse 10

But my horn shalt thou exalt like the horn of an uni-
corn: I shall be anointed with fresh oil.

DROWNING VOICES POEM

I'm drowning,
I'm drowning in my own voice,
Feeling like I don't really get a choice,
Living my life,
Thinking about my past strife,
Will I ever even get a wife?
Thinking about memories,
My stories,
My own fury.

I'm drowning,
Not only in my own voice but the voices of the lost,
The voices that cost,
The voices that give you so much chill you frost,

I'm always hearing voices,
The voices of those who doubt me,
Voices of those who don't know me,
The voices that think they own me,
Just cause I'm kind to thee,
Don't mean you can trample what you see,

Sometimes I wish I heard your voice,
Wish you had a choice,
But when the voices bring sorrow,
You can only borrow,
And follow what you don't know.

I keep drowning in my own voice,
Talking,
Chatting,
never stopping,
Repeating...repeating...repeating

Wishing someone could hear me,
Hear not what you see,
But what is within me,
Within thee,
The soul that she could see,
Not what she wanted me to be,
But who I was even when everybody wanted to flee.

I keep drowning,
Drowning,
Frowning,
Keep on mounting,
Mounting...
even crawling,
till you can fly,
don't cry,
at least try,
Try to fly,
My oh my,
To die,

Not to fly,
Ending with nothing left
me mory,
His tory,
Her story,
My story,
Our story,
Cause leaving without creating is my greatest fear,
I try not to steer,
Try not to peer,
Or wish too dear,
Try not to smear,
What you are creating
And leave the wheel to the God who keeps relating,
Who you keep debating,
Which keeps you derailing,
Never staying,
Replacing...
defacing

Voice lost,
At what cost?
Not my portion,
Cause I got a voice I have to speak,
It's my destiny,
A little bit chaotic with frenzy,
But still my destiny,
My presidency,
My residency,
Cause they may get tired of my voice,
Get tired of my choice,
But aint no way I am losing my voice,
They try to destroy,

But I use it to rejoice,
And no way I'm losing my joy,
Cause it aint no toy,
And I am a boy,
Who is growing up to be a man,
with a voice,
and a choice.

ACKNOWLEDGEMENTS

Thank you to those who helped me find light within the Darkness, Laughter within the Storm, Hope within the Hardships, and giving me space when I'm writing. Because you all know that is my sacred zone.

I am sincerely grateful to my Christ the King School family for broadening my poetic perspective on the world.

Another gratitude goes to my Colchester High School family for helping me never shy away from the hard conversations in Society, and helping me find my growing voice in a world of change

Thank you to all my Teachers and Friends y'all have impacted me in more ways than can be expressed, only through my poetry can you find this out.

Thank you to my church for being a light

Edonusem H.A.Y. Pomeyie is an author who wrote his first book at the age of 12 titled "Poems of My Understanding." As a Ghanaian boy raised in the land of opportunity he has accomplished many things which include his two time Vermont speech all state Performance Poetry tournament win, and many district and all state music performances. Edonusem currently goes to Colchester High School where he is well known for his big smile and his vivacious personality. He loves to read and write poetry, play ball while pursuing music, and watching medical shows in his free time. He is a Christian and aspires to be a gospel musician and medical doctor in the future.